EXPERIENCE GOD WITHOUT RELIGION

A pragmatic's guide to
encountering the Divine
in seven basic steps

DENIS POISSON

Copyright © 2011 Denis Poisson

All rights reserved

No part of this publication may be reproduced, distributed, or transmitted in any form or by any means, including photocopying, recording, or other electronic or mechanical methods, without the prior written permission of the author, except in the case of brief quotations embodied in critical reviews and certain other non commercial uses permitted by copyright law.

For permission requests, please e-mail the author, completing the subject field with "Attention: Permissions Coordinator," to denis@thekeymakers.co.uk

The right of Denis Poisson to be identified as the author of this work has been asserted by him in accordance with Copyright, Designs and Patents Act, 1988

ISBN: 978-1-4478-1409-2

For William

CONTENTS

Foreword

Introduction

Step 1: What God Isn't

Step 2: What God Is

Step 3: The Hypothalamus

Step 4: Disbelief

Step 5: Keep it secret

Step 6: Surrender

Step 7: Taking it Further

Bibliography

Foreword

Welcome to the part of the book that usually gets skipped.

I'm sorry, I really wasn't expecting anyone to read this bit, and yet here you are, happily reading away.

I'll try to use the opportunity to say something useful.

Maybe something about religion to start off with.

More precisely, your religion or absence of religion and how compatible it may be with the ideas explored in this book.

I know it's probably a worry.

Don't worry, I've done my homework.

The ideas, steps and exercises presented in this book are all 100% compatible with your beliefs, whatever they may be.

You can be atheist, Christian, Muslim, Jewish, Buddhist, Hindu, Sikh, or Pagan and every one of these pages will still be useful to you and in line with what you already believe.

Now, the fact that you have picked this book up tells me that you have either:

never had a religious experience or

you have had one or two but have found it hard to get back to that experience.

If you fall into one of these two categories, this book is for you.

The techniques you will read about appear in all the great traditions we just mentioned, I've just stripped down the mystical aspects and presented them in their raw form.

This book will give you nothing but the basics. It'll be up to you whether you want to dress them up afterwards with the additional trappings of any religion of you choice.

A word of warning though: you're about to read a number of words over the course of this book, and I'm worried that you may not like some of them.

Like for example the word 'God'.

The trouble is that misinformation and misunderstanding have plagued the word 'God' for centuries.

A lot of people don't like the word 'God' and don't want anything to do with what it represents for them.

I've done my best to interchange it with the expression 'the Divine', but the truth is that you could replace the word with something altogether more appropriate if you wished.

It's just that there's this thing that this book helps you get in contact with, and we just need a word to talk about it.

So, I'll sometimes just use the word 'God' for short. I promise we'll define that though. It's not necessarily the 'God' you're thinking of.

Finally, let me thank you, dear reader.

By picking up this book you have proven that you actually do want more than the child-friendly simplifications offered by most 'religious' books, but you also want something a little more engaging and accessible than an academic journal.

You are in good hands, I have no doubt that your trust will be rewarded over the following pages and days as we head into this very strange spiritual territory.

Spirituality isn't something to be studied. It's something to be experienced. As you are about to find out.

I wish you every success on the way.

Introduction

Let me take you on a little journey back in time, just twelve years back, to a horrid little place on the East coast of England called Clacton-on-sea. (I can see the look on your face, and I don't blame you. This book gets better, I promise.)

On the sea front, there's an old red-brick Victorian hotel. It's a huge building overlooking the sea and must have been a very nice place when it was first built.

As we approach, we can notice a billboard announcing that the hotel is currently being used as a campus for the Colchester Institute of Anglia University, a training place for future hotel managers and a handful of leisure and tourism students.

This is where bright young faces fresh out of secondary school go to waste away if their career advisor is as talented as mine was.

Just to the left of this rather grand ex-hotel is a huge, crumbling white box-shaped building with tiny windows and an iron-framed, single-glazed front door.

Very 1960's.

That's the halls of residence where most of the drink in the world gets drunk and most of the dope in the universe gets smoked. Let's get a bit closer... through the door and up the winding staircase to the first floor. Past the common room where a couple of students seem to have fallen asleep (what else is there to do here?...), through the fire doors, and... ah! Here we are.

First room on the left.

This is my room. Twelve years ago.

Let's enter.

It's my room.

I don't mind.

Come in.

There I am, sitting on my bed, spliff in one hand, a Bible in the other.

I'm not Christian. In fact, I don't believe in God at all at this time, so I'm certainly not reading the Bible out of duty.

I'm reading it because I'm curious: I believe that the idea of a big white-bearded man in the sky is preposterous, and I want to find out more about the book where this nonsense supposedly came from.

Except that's not at all what I'm finding so far.

Let's see... I seem to have already read quite a chunk, looks like I'm well into the fourth quarter. (It's amazing the amount of free time a student who isn't enjoying his course can find...)

Now, take a look at my face... I look puzzled. And it doesn't seem to be the dope's fault.

The open page has lots of red pen scribbling in the margins. Question marks, underlined sentences... What's that written in tiny red letters there? 'Don't understand this... why?' Same as most of the preceding pages then...

I read a little further, the puzzled look turns to surprise, and then vague recognition. I look a little nervous, but determined.

I climb off the bed go to lock the door.

I get down on my knees and start talking... what... to myself? Doesn't look like it...

I look... relieved. In fact I look pretty happy.

Grateful.

Ok, guys, enough of the guided tour, let's leave me to it.

Welcome back to wherever you were before you started reading. What you just witnessed was me having my first time ever religious experience.

Was I talking to Jesus? No. Jesus' teachings helped me understand how to talk to God (as defined in Steps 1 and 2), not to him.

Did I convert to Christianity? No. Not to anything most Christians would call Christianity, anyway.

Did I convert to any other religion? No, though I did start studying other religions and finding similarities between them.

Did the experience change my life? Yes, I can't begin to tell you how much, but I will give you some examples over the next few chapters.

Did it make me stop believing in the usefulness of science? No. I am still sane.

Did it make me believe that the world was created in seven days? No. My brain didn't suddenly drop out, I am still able to differentiate between metaphor and natural science.

Did I start going to church after that? Well, yes, but not for long: Other people told me I should because I'd found Jesus' teachings useful... But what I found in churches (dogma, repetition and sometimes pure folly) had nothing to do with the life-enhancing teachings I'd found in the Bible and then subsequently in other 'sacred' scriptures. So I stopped going. Religion and God were clearly two separate things.

Did it prompt me to find out more about how religious experiences work? Yes.

Could I go back to living without the constant help of what I call 'God' or 'the Divine' (though others call it Mind-at-Large, YHWH, Allah – which is the Arabic word for 'the Almighty' –, the Tao, the Universe, the Force and many other things too...)? Sure, but why would I want to? In the same way I could live without a mobile phone, but I can't imagine choosing to.

After twelve years of research into the histories of religions, as well as their original teachings and scriptures, did I find answers? Yes, many.

This book is about some of those answers. It's amazing what you discover if you're interested enough and you don't have an organisation threatening you with Hell for being nosy...

I believe that religious or spiritual experiences are not magical or mystical.

I believe that they are not the exclusive property of 'religious' people. I believe that you don't have to belong to a special 'club' in order to encounter the Divine, but that many organisations make a lot of money from being a 'one-size-fits-all' shoehorn through which most people fail to have any experience at all.

Twelve years of research has forced me to conclude that *anyone* can have a religious experience.

Whoever you are, that includes you.

To this day, most people who are lucky enough to stumble across a religious experience do so by chance, and then they naturally become devout followers of whatever religion is dominant in their part of the world, because it seems to be able to explain what they experienced.

Unfortunately with that often comes the idea that "my religion is the only ***true*** religion and other *'false'* religions must be stopped for the good of mankind so that everyone can have this perfect thing that I have."

I mean, it's understandable: divine experiences change your life so radically and so profoundly for the better that anyone who's had one will want everyone else to have one too.

This is where this book fits in.

I want to dispel the idea that religious experiences have anything to do with allegiance to one religion or another.

Religions are merely languages with which to talk about these out-of-the-ordinary experiences.

And now, with a little information, a dab of biology, a little pinch of psychology, and the tiniest dash of metaphysics thrown in for good measure, you can have a religious experience too.

If you want one that is...

This book is to be taken as a whole. There are seven steps which must be used *together*. They are not seven ways to have a religious experience, they are one way divided into seven sections.

You can start on any of the steps, though I think that the order in which they are presented here makes most sense.

Be prepared for some strangeness, but hopefully no requests for any ridiculous leaps of faith.

So if you think you're ready, I'll see you on the next page for Step 1.

STEP 1

WHAT GOD ISN'T

Having a religious experience *should* be a simple affair.

The trouble is that a number of barriers tend to get in the way.

The steps in this book should help you overcome those barriers giving you an open route to what you're looking for.

The first step in any journey is to have an idea of the destination.

The first barrier preventing most people from having a religious experience is the fact that they already have an idea of what the destination *should* be, or what they would *like* the destination to be like, which doesn't necessarily match the *actual* destination that is available.

The trouble is, giving an accurate description of what the Divine is (and what our destination is) isn't straightforward.

Let me explain:

A couple of weeks ago, my three-year old nephew asked me what a pterodactyl was.

I was able to explain that it was like a big lizard with leathery wings that lived millions of years ago.

It was a good description, and it worked because we both knew what a lizard is and what leather is like and how long a year lasts.

Simple

Compare that with our case now.

At this point - before you have had your first encounter with the Divine - there's very little from your normal everyday life that we use for comparison.

That's why so many people get the wrong idea about what the Divine *should* be and then get lost searching for something that just isn't there.

I'm not saying it's impossible to describe the Divine, just that it might require a little more patience and imagination than it would to describe a pterodactyl.

Let's start with what the Divine is *not*.

Throughout this book, there will be short action plans for you to engage in. After all, you don't want to just *read* about religious experiences, do you?

You want to experience one for yourself.

That's why you picked up this book.

Completing these practical tasks will get you there.

I would suggest that skipping over them would be like reading about how to swim without ever wanting to get wet feet.

These 'practice' sections are your chance to splash right in.

Practice 1

1) Grab a pen and a jot-pad, (If you don't have a jot pad, the back of any old envelope or micro-meal packaging you salvaged from the recycling bin will do.)

2) Write down everything you think God is probably like.

3) Put the list down.

4) Now think of a young child you know, old enough to talk. Imagine they're describing you to a friend. Now let's say their friend wrote a list of the things they knew about you based on what they'd heard. How much of that list is likely to be accurate about the real you? How much of it would just be way off the mark? If you told them that some of it was inaccurate, how likely would they be to be able to pinpoint what was incorrect without help?

5) Now look at your list about God. What's correct? What's incorrect?

6) Re-watch 'Avatar', or just fast forward to the scene where the guy asks the girl to teach him, and the girl answers that she can't fill a cup that is already full. If you're not an Avatar fan, check out the exact same scene in the awful '2012', (really? 2012 rather than Avatar?) or again in the slightly less awful 'The Forbidden Kingdom' (Jacky Chan Vs. Jet Lee, oh yes!).

7) Emptying your cup is an exercise in humility, a quality that didn't exactly come naturally to me.... You may be able to do it today, but if you find it difficult, at least decide that you want to. Realising that we don't really know may be uncomfortable, but it is necessary work which will open the way to the next gate. (It doesn't either mean that all we know is wrong, just that there might be more to learn.)

8) Repeat to yourself that it's ok not to know everything.

I have no pretention of knowing everything either, but by the time you have finished this book, you will hopefully be in hands that are much more competent than mine in this respect. Better to get it directly from the source, eh? That's what I thought too.

Now we started this chapter by suggesting that we needed to shed false expectations, so here is a short list of what the Divine definitely *isn't*.

'Not the God of the philosophers and scholars'

In 1654, a Mathematician/ Philosopher you may have heard of called Blaise Pascal had a religious experience. In his diary, he recorded the event like this:

"23 November 1654, between 10:30 and 12:30pm.

Fire.

God of Abraham, God of Isaac, God of Jacob, not of the philosophers and the scholars..."

Psacal clearly found it important to point out what this God he'd encountered was *not*: '...*not of the philosophers and the scholars...*'

Scholars and philosophers such as Thomas Aquinas, Saint Augustine and more recently William Paley have used 'logic' (of dubious merit) to prove the existence of God for centuries.

I believe they have done more harm than good while exposing themselves to counter-arguments and mostly ridicule.

Trying to explain the Divine with logic is like trying to explain a music festival with mathematics. Fascinating to a few as self-satisfying intellectual exercise maybe, but it would miss the point entirely!

You could prove the existence of colour to a blind person using logic, but what would be the use? What matters is the *experience* of colour, not the belief that it exists... What's more, if the blind person were to recover sight, would their experience of colour be in any way similar to their previous understanding of colour? Of course not. How could it?

The Divine, in the same way as colour, love, déjà-vu, or Ben and Jerry's Fairly Nuts ice-cream are things you just can't accurately describe with logic. You have to experience them.

So when I use the word 'God' or 'The Divine', I'm not talking about 'the God of philosophers and scholars' either. God is a raw, immediate experience. Not a concept.

God isn't a 'he' or a 'she'.

The second inaccuracy I need to point out is the idea that the Divine is a person. I know many people think of God as an imaginary friend, like a big, invisible wizard or something.

I think I know why:

Most people stop trying to learn about God around age 10 when the abstract mind is only just barely kicking in. The enduring Zeus image is nice and easy to understand if not easy (or sane) for an educated adult to 'believe in'.

For this reason, I will avoid calling God 'Him' or 'He' throughout this book. I just don't think it's helpful.

I know that these words were never meant to suggest that God was male rather than female; the capital 'H' in 'He' points to a fourth category altogether:

not an 'it',

not a 'she'

not a 'he',

God is a '**He**'...

but too few people know this which is why I try to avoid using a pronoun at all.

So the Divine is not bound by gender or indeed by any form, human or other. A bit like memory or sleep.

<u>God isn't a cruel Victorian work-house matron</u>

Our society's natural tendency is to expect God to be a punishing bully who will make you pay eternal suffering for having been 'offensive'. Isn't that what our main Judeo-Christian institutions have told us for centuries?

Here's an analogy that gives a clearer picture in my opinion:

Say you're a very small child and your parent/guardian warns you not touch the oven shelf because it's hot. Now, say you decided to disobey and touch it anyway... Would the resulting burn have anything to do with your parent/guardian 'punishing' you?

Now about Heaven and Hell...

You may be surprised to read that I do believe in Heaven and Hell, but not as magical places in the clouds and underground, in fact not as actual *places* at all. And certainly not as a *reward* or *punishment* for deeds performed; as an experience that happens as a natural consequence of making certain choices however... well why not.

If I do something helpful or kind or selfless, I feel good, if I do something selfish, cruel or hateful, I feel bad.

It's not rocket science.

Heaven and Hell are experiences that happen naturally following certain choices.

Ever heard someone say something like 'The poor thing's in a really bad place at the moment, can't stop crying...' You can experience these to some extent in your everyday waking state.

For now, I'll just say that if I knew God to be this tyrant who dishes out brownie points or trips to the naughty corner when the game's over I'd be writing a book about how to protect ourselves from God, not one about how to get closer!

God doesn't have favourites

That's right.

No favourites. At all. Not even Oprah Winfrey.

No particular group of people, (religious or not), no particular nationality, but also, I believe, no particular species or even particular forms of life.

If it's part of the Universe, then it's part of the Divine, and God wants what's best for it.

I can tell some of you are protesting... 'Why does God reward those who follow the right religion and punish those who don't?'

Who says that's the case? The religions themselves? 'Bit convenient, wouldn't you say...?

God isn't what you've been taught by religious leaders

One of the sentences that caught my attention when I read the Bible (as an Atheist) for the first time was:

> *'Woe to you, teachers of the law and Pharisees, you hypocrites! You travel over land and sea to win a single convert, and when he becomes one, you make him twice as much a son of hell as you are.'*
>
> *Matthew 23:15*

When I first read that I thought: 'That's exactly why I've never wanted anything to do with religions.'

If you only take one thing away from this book, let it be that no-one can tell you what God is like.

Except for me...

JOKING!!! Completely joking. Come back...

I can only help you experience God.

Only you can find out what God is like.

God is an experience that every single living being can encounter. That experience is unique to each and every one of us.

So keep on reading and get your own understanding of what God is like. Not mine, not anyone else's.

Just yours.

Practice 2

1) Get that list of what you thought God was like and compare it to the list you just read of what God is definitely not like. Is that still ok? Do you still want to have a divine encounter

2) Now jot down anything I've said so far that doesn't sound sensible to you so that you can come back to it later.

It's ok, I'm really not going anywhere, you'll be able to find me exactly where you leave me when you get back from grabbing that notepad and a pen again (or page from the printer, or mirror and lipstick, or cave wall and lump of charcoal, or mobile phone's note page, whatever you have!).

Go for it.

Ok. Now write down what doesn't seem right in what you've just read (if anything), and I'll see you on the next page for step 2.

STEP 2

What God Is

If you're reading these lines, I'll assume that you're comfortable with what you've read so far and you agree that you can't find out what God is like until you experience the Divine directly for yourself.

Great. It's finally safe to make some attempts at talking about what God *is* like without running the risk of you thinking it's going to be accurate.

A word of warning, though, this second step is full of freaky ideas and bizarre conclusions, mainly to get you thinking about what reality is.

It really isn't the end of the world if you don't enjoy it and want to move on. If it gets too much, just jump to Step 3 for some good hard science. It would be a shame to miss this though; for me, this is the interesting part, the bit where we get to step through the looking glass... Once you're in, there's no turning back!

The moon, not the finger

There's a nice Chinese proverb you may have heard that goes:

'When the wise man points to the moon, the fool looks at the finger'.

I can only point from here.

Just remember that the finger isn't the Moon. The following description is (and can only ever be) a pointer to set you in a general direction, and not the thing itself.

Anyway, here we go.

Know thyself, who art in God's image.

People from various traditions have suggested that we are made in God's likeness.

That suggests that if we could know what we were really like, we could make more accurate guesses at what God might be like too. Investigating what we're really like is the purpose of this chapter.

Obviously (by now, I hope) we're not going to talk about what we look like physically, because that's not the clue we're looking for. As we have mentioned, God isn't a big humanoid in the sky.

We're not going to look at what our personality is like either. Personality is what makes us individual, different from one another.

No. We need to look at our common traits, things we share with all other sentient beings (not just humans). Like awareness. Consciousness. Mind.

What is Mind?

Mind is where everything happens.

Now the following crazy proposition is something you already know, which is good because I'm not going to need to do any convincing.

But while you know it, you may not have thought about it in this way before. Apologies for any brains I manage to scramble along the way.

Try your hand at the following brain-masher. See what I mean.

Practice 3

Read the following six points, They may seem counter-intuitive, but can you positively prove the contrary?

1) **All of our experience happens in our brain. It is informed by our five senses, but the *experience* happens inside our brain.**

2) **A regular CT scan will reveal that different experiences are manifested in different regions of the brain.**

3) **What we call 'the real world' really does seem to be 'out there'. The illusion is perfect until you think about it methodically:**

4) **Your eyes are not windows. We get the *impression* that our mind peers out of our eyes at the outside world, as if our eyes were transparent window panes, but any primary school kid can tell you that our eyes are actually receptors, sensors which *relay* information to our brain. Light hits our retina, and the optic nerve sends the**

signal to our brain. The signals are decoded by our brain and immediately interpreted as an image... which is the image we *actually* get to see! So whatever you think you're seeing, you are actually only seeing a reproduction of it, inside your brain. The only image you can access is the image that your brain has created for you from the information that the optical nerve has sent it.

5) If there *is* indeed a 'real' world out there on which your brain-generated image is based, you will never be able to apprehend it directly. For all we know, the eye itself may be a construct of the brain... Wait, might it be possible that the brain itself is a construct of the 'brain'? Which leaves us with what? Pure Mind-at-Large?

6) So there is only one thing of which you can be *sure:* that the things you experience exist within your mind. Of course, it's generally agreed by sane people that they are truly based on an actual reality 'out there'. It's certainly the

way things are set up to appear, but can we *prove* it? Of course you could ask someone else if they are seeing the same thing, but wait... where does that 'other person' exist?

These words on the page... you can see them?

They are in your mind.

Look around you now.

Everything you see is only the reflection that your brain is creating based on the signals your retinas and optical nerves are sending you.

Everything you see is in your mind.

So where is your mind?

Reason tells us 'in our brain'...

...but is it not conceivable that it is our brain which is in our mind?

See if you can prove the opposite.

The same applies to hearing.

We all know about the eardrums that beat out frequencies that our brain interprets as sounds, yet we normally get the impression that we are hearing the sound itself... We know that isn't the case.

We only ever experience our brain's *interpretation* of the signal. We never get to experience the signal itself.

(Of course, despite initial appearances, I'm not completely insane, so as a rule I base my life on the *belief* that all these things I perceive in my mind *are indeed* reflections of real things 'out there', it's the belief that seems to work best most of the time when I'm trying to survive on a day-to-day basis; but once in a while, it's good to remember that it is nothing more than a *belief* that can be ditched for a new perspective when useful...)

Hopefully by this time, you're either feeling pretty smug at having worked all this out before (we should hang out!), or you are completely freaked out which is great (enjoy it!), or you are basking in delight which is also great, or your head is spinning and you feel sick from the mental work-out, in which case, put the book down, take a rest, and think about it from time to time over the next few days, relaxed in the knowledge that you're in the majority (see you in Step 3 when you're ready!)

I just think it's useful to remind ourselves that '*real*' is a tricky word.

Ok, those of you who are still with me, let's push on.

How big is your Mind?

Of course, the contents of our mind doesn't end with what our five 'external' senses feed us…

Can you think of the place you last went on holiday to?

So I guess that's in your mind too.

Can you think of China? Or a country you've never been to?

So that's in your mind too…

What about the Moon? The Milky Way? Further?

If all of this is contained within your mind, how big is your mind?

Check it out for yourself…

Look for a limit…

Can you find one?

Is there a limit to your mind in space?

What about in time?

Can you think about what you did yesterday evening? What about dinosaurs? All in there?

Whatever is contained in your mind is your Universe. Your World.

If my Mind is infinite, where do other people fit in?

Have you ever had a dream in which you featured as one of the characters?

All of that dream happened inside your mind, you won't deny that, right?

You didn't 'go' to a magical land in the clouds, you just experienced stuff that your mind was constructing for you at the time.

Effectively, you (lying in your bed) were the mind within which the scene took place; everything in that dream took place inside of your mind…

…including the character of 'you' that featured in the dream.

The version of you in the dream were a construct of your own mind.

But what about the other protagonists?

Also inside your mind!

It's obvious to you now you're awake, but at the time you were experiencing it? They certainly *seemed* like separate entities…

What about in waking life then?

Could there be a higher level of 'reality' in which we will realise that all our friends and enemies in the so-called 'waking world' were actually just aspects of ourselves?

We are all One

There's a great Buddhist metaphor which speaks of a net ('Indra's net') which is as vast as the universe, and woven into this net, at every knot where the threads intersect, there is a polished jewel which reflects all the other jewels in the net.

The metaphor refers to us. You/I/we are the jewel and the reflection of the other jewels too.

I think many people have had direct experiences of the Divine, and as the example that I followed to reach my own, I hold Jesus in high regard.

Some people suggest that he may never have existed, to which I answer that I don't particularly care: the teachings and example attributed to him showed me the way.

What more could I ask for?

In the Bible's New Testament, when the Pharisees asked him which was the greatest commandment from the Old Testament (of which there are 613!), he answered:

1) *'Hear, O Israel, the LORD your God, the LORD is one.*
2) *Love your God with all your heart and all your strength and all your soul and all your mind.*
3) *And the second is like it: Love your neighbour as yourself.'*

Let's dissect that a little: Jesus is asked for the one greatest commandment, and he comes up with three:

1) *Love God,*
2) *Love your neighbour,*
3) *Love yourself.*

(By the way, he doesn't say 'Love your neighbour *as much* as you love yourself, but rather: 'Love your neighbour *as* yourself.'

As your actual *self*.)

I think we have two clues here as to what he meant which can be useful in your quest for a religious experience.

The first clue is six little words that link it all up: '...and the second is like it...'

Jesus is saying that *'Love your neighbour as yourself'* is like *'Love your God'*.

It means the same thing (Google the parable of the sheep and the goats if you need more convincing).

But the second clue I think is the clincher: 'The LORD is One'.

There's a nice Hindu story about a little boy who comes back from Spiritual Instruction to his mother after learning that God and he are one and the same thing. He gets home and goes straight for the expensive china cabinet where he picks out the nicest china dish and smashes it on the floor, upon which he climbs down from the stool, plants both feet firmly on the ground, crosses his arms and smirks defiantly at his mother. His mother remains calm and asks him what that was about.

'Do you know who I am?' he smiles.

His mother has been to her own spiritual Instruction classes as a girl and guesses what this week's topic might have been.

'Ah,' she nods smiling and understanding. 'You're God.'

'Correct!' cries the triumphant child 'We're all God!'

'But tell me,' continues the mother, 'If you are Little Boy God, then that makes me Big Mummy God. What a bad Mummy God I'd be if I let my Little Boy God go thinking he could just go around smashing china plates!'

And so Little Boy God got a good hiding!

Beyond the slapstick comedy value, the story points out the important implication that the fact that we are 'in God's image' means that we have great responsibilities.

Practise 4

This is not necessarily one for jotting down, rather one for thinking about:

What are you?

Your body belongs to you, but if you were to lose some of it you would still be 'you'...

Your thoughts?

Once again, generated by you but not actually you...

So what is that deep, profound thing you call 'I' when you say things like 'I am'...?

That formless, timeless, limitless essence of existence that you have in common with all other beings.

Deeper than just the way you appear to the five external senses...

That is what is in the likeness of God.

If you found this chapter a little tough to chew on, don't sweat.

As I mentioned before, the next step involves no crazy ideas, just science (ok, a few crazy ideas, but nothing this mad!).

See you there!

STEP 3

THE HYPOTHALAMUS

Here comes the science...

Isn't the hypothalamus great?

It's the sentence I normally break the ice with at parties.

My wife says it's the main reason why I usually end up standing alone in a corner trying to look cool. I don't normally get invited back.

Isn't the hypothalamus great though?...

Sorry, what's that?

Can't quite remember what the hypothalamus is?

Hey no problem.

Here's a reminder.

The hypothalamus is the area at the back of your brain which controls things like body temperature, hunger, thirst, sleep, and other stuff like that.

In other words, it makes sure that you do what's necessary to keep your body alive rather than spend day after day lost in metaphysical thought.

It does another thing too: the hypothalamus acts as a barrier against any information from your internal and external world that's not immediately essential to your survival.

It ensures that at any one moment you have just enough information to cope with and to keep you alive.

So it keeps out anything that's not related to the survival of your biological body, and it lets in stuff like 'This area seems safe for sleeping', 'That food smells rancid', 'OMG! IT'S A BEAR! RUN!' and any other similarly helpful titbits that might help you stay alive and comfortable.

So we agree, our hypothalamus is a pretty useful part of our brain and we can be grateful for it.

Only there's a catch:

It *never* takes a break. Well... rarely, anyway.

Sure, if it didn't work at least some of the time, we would forget to feed /hydrate /protect (etc.) ourselves and die; but wouldn't it be nice to be allowed to switch it off for a short period of time?

Just once in a while?

Let a little 'non-essential' data in?

Experience a little more than just eat-drink-sleep-remove discomfort-reproduce?

The good news is that an 'off' switch *does* exist.

Here are some well known techniques that let you access that switch.

1 - Fasting

There are no major world religions that don't include a time of fasting.

By fasting, I don't mean giving up chocolate as some pious church-goers might do for Lent.

I'm not saying that giving up something you like isn't an admirable thing to do, or even a spiritually useful thing to do; I'm just saying that that sort of thing should come under 'Sacrifice', not 'Fasting' – more on sacrifice later.

Fasting means eating little or nothing.

What's the point I hear you say? Well, I promised to stay away from mystic nonsense psychobabble and stick with the scientific facts for this chapter, so here's a short-sweet-and-easy biology primer:

The hypothalamus, that brain area that filters reality, runs on sugar (among other things). Starve it and it stops working as a barrier, letting the floodgates of perception burst wide open, giving free pass to the full extent of the human experience, including all information, from raw uninhibited emotions, to God.

Simple as that.

Have a think about any religion that you are even vaguely familiar with and think if there are times when its practitioners are required to avoid eating.

If that religion's current form doesn't demand periods of fasting, do a little research to find out if it used to. Fasting is required for a good reason.

I was interested to find out for example that in some strictly Catholic countries like Poland, church-goers aren't allowed to eat or drink on Christmas eve before they return from mass. The same applies at Easter!

2 – Singing

Another fuel that the hypothalamus needs a good supply of is oxygen. Low oxygen means low hypothalamus activity and once again the effects mentioned above can kick in.

Now let's take a second to imagine you holding your breath for a couple of minutes.

Imagine I said!

Right. How would that feel?

Panic? Terror? Longing for breath?

All these emotions are hardly going to help you achieve the peace and openness you'd need to enjoy the experience.

So how can you reduce the amount of oxygen in your body without the panic attack getting in the way?

The answer's simple.

Singing.

Now if you're anything like me, (and don't worry, I'm not saying you are...!) your singing *will* produce panic attacks; mine does, but only for those listening to me. I'm usually fine.

If you're the same, that's ok.

Producing panic attacks in other people is allowed. Celine Dion has made a long successful career of it and she's still going.

And it really doesn't matter what you sing.

Whether it's repetitive, hypnotic chants like those used by most traditional Eastern, Native American, Australasian and African traditions, or more elaborate hymns and songs of praise that have been composed for churches (more aesthetically pleasing but much less effective), it makes no difference, as long as it's heartfelt, involving and prolonged.

From a phenomenological point of view, the very modern practice found in certain churches of 'speaking in tongues' amounts to nothing more than singing without the inconvenience of having to remember words, a tune or even having to make any sense at all!

Unlike the 'tongues' spoken by the apostles at Pentecost (which could be interpreted by foreign passers-by who were astonished to hear their own language spoken in Galilee,) the 'speaking in tongues' heard in modern charismatic churches consists of fervent babbling of whatever sounds come naturally to the speaker, ensuring a near-uninterrupted flow of expelled air.

But this modern version of 'speaking in tongues' has a very useful purpose: that of getting the hypothalamus' filter out of the way, so I would be the last to condemn its demonstrably practical use.

Evangelical Christians who have used this practice will know from experience how effective it is at creating a stronger feeling of involvement with the rest of the religious ceremony.

(As an aside for readers who would insist that actually, speaking in tongues really *is* a supernatural gift, and that just because no one in the congregation can interpret it, doesn't mean it's not an actual language...

I have personally experienced standing in a Pentecostal church, and heard these so-called 'foreign languages' which for some reason only seem to consist of three syllables.

There are only so many permutations and meanings possible for '*Aaaah-golo-golo-golo-golo-golo-golo-goloooooh! Aaaah-golo-golo-golo-golo-golo-*

golo-golo-goloooob!' Sunday after Sunday, week after week, year in, year out...

And yet the 'speakers of tongues' continue to do it.

Why?

Not to feel left out?

No.

It genuinely does something for them.

Something physical, resulting in a detachment from the physical world and making the following teachings, rites and practices infinitely more meaningful, as it is in this state that they are meant to be experienced.

Surely that's good enough a reason to continue with the practice, is there really a need to insist that it's a real language?)

3 – Breathing

If you've understood the section above about singing, then this should be self-explanatory. It's the same thing for the non-musical.

Pranayama breathing exercises popular in certain Yogic practises (notably Hatha and Raja Yoga) have exactly this effect.

The Hindu sacred text Baghavad Gita mentions pranayama which is translated: *'trance induced by stopping all breathing'*.

I suppose that if it is practiced in the context of religious discipline it may be accompanied by the necessary calm without which trying to attain a spiritual experience is futile.

Pranayama exercises are easy to find online, here's a simple one though, touted as the 'most popular yoga exercise': it's called Sudharshan Chakra Kriya.

But if you prefer to call it 'holding your breath for a long time', feel free to do so. It's not quite as poetic, or as exotic to Western ears, but I suppose that's the price you pay for stripping down religious practices of their mystical airs to get to the core of what's really happening.

You win some you lose some.

If you're interested, this is how Sudharshan Chakra Kriya is done: you sit in the Lotus position, or whatever position happens to be most comfortable for you while maintaining a straight, upright back (What's that? You say you find sitting in a chair more comfortable than the Lotus position? What's wrong with you? Are you telling me you haven't spent your life sitting on the floor leading you to find the Lotus position to be the most comfortable position of all? What is the world coming to, eh?)

Anyway, once you're in your comfortable upright position (on a chair), you block one nostril and inhale.

Holding your breath, you pump your stomach muscles in and out 16 times (keep that breath held in!), repeating all the while, silently in your head, 'Wahe Guru', or 'Allahu Akhbar', or 'Hallelujah' or 'Don't forget to get bread and milk', or any other sentence that helps you find peace. (It gives you something to focus on while your body is slowly drained of oxygen and your hypothalamus is gently shut down opening you to a more complete experience of reality. Truth be told, your shopping list might just be one of the weaker examples...)

And then breath out.

And repeat.

Are you seeing a pattern here?

Apart from stars behind your eyelids?

4 - Self-mutilation

(Definitely not my favorite, but interesting to know nonetheless.)

If you've read the DaVinci Code, you'll know about the practice of self-mutilation.

The 'cilice' mentioned in the novel is widely used by people who practice self-mutilation, but to be honest, any form of physical hardship can be used to raise adrenaline levels, which is the fourth method of affecting the hypothalamus.

The body takes over and the mind gives way to much deeper, more primeval senses.

I wouldn't recommend this method, though self-harmers can become addicted to its effects, as may extreme sports adepts.

The same process happens in fast rides at theme parks and fairs. Until you get used to them, that is.

5 – Tampering directly with your brain

For information only, obviously, though I feel I should mention it for the sake of completeness.

I would not recommend this any more than I would recommend self-mutilation, but there is a shortcut to switching off the hypothalamus effectively called 'mescaline'.

It is an illegal extract from the Peyote cactus, also found in some other cacti.

I won't go into the details of how mescaline disables the human hypothalamus here given the wealth of information that you can find online, and if you're that into it, you've probably already read Aldous Huxley's ***The Doors of Perception*** and ***Heaven and Hell*** to which I can add nothing.

There you have it. A complete guide to pressing the pause button on your hypothalamus and letting a bit more reality in.

Practise 5

1) *Next time you feel hungry, notice how much less you interact with the outside world... notice how your thoughts turn inward and your inner voice becomes clearer.*

2) *Try chanting. It doesn't matter what you chant, though the things you say affect your conscious and your unconscious mind. Chanting about gratitude for your life and love for the Universe might be more useful than chanting about what you think of the opposite team, though the effects do overlap...*

3) *Try a yogic breathing exercise. There are plenty you can find videos for online.*

4) *Make a note of which one you like best, you'll use it for your own religious experience by the end of this book.*

Our third step is now covered: take down that hypothalamus firewall.

We are making progress.

I have to break it to you at some point though:

Taking down that wall isn't enough, particularly since there is a second, even greater wall right behind it which we'll deal with in Step 4.

STEP 4

DISBELIEF

I won't dwell too long on this one.

The second, greater firewall is disbelief.

Too obvious?

Again, if it's not something you struggle with then consider yourself lucky and in the minority. See you in Step 5!

To the rest of us who find it not only difficult but downright absurd to believe something with no evidence, let me offer some help.

Keep the baby, ditch the bathwater

First off, a little reminder that I'm not suggesting for one second that you need to believe in what mainstream popular culture calls 'God'.

I'm not either asking you to believe in a resurrected imaginary friend.

And you certainly don't have to stop believing in sound, sensible notions such as evolution or the fact that the world has been around for more than 6000 years.

There's this small Indian sect whose adepts still believe that the world is flat. They believe that it is supported on the backs of four elephants that stand on the shell of a giant turtle who swims around the Universe.

These people also believe that it is wrong to harm animals.

Well, I happen to agree with that second belief.

I would also say that it would probably be ok for me adopt that belief without necessarily having to also embrace the flat-world theory just because it happens to be included in the same package...

In the same way, it should be perfectly legitimate to believe that religious experiences actually do happen to people of sound mind without them having to also believe that the world was created in 7 days by an old man in the sky (which, contrary to what the media would have us believe is a view shared by only a tiny proportion of the Christian world, since most Christians actually own a brain of their own and are educated in the art of using it. I guess the media isn't so interested in sane people though...)

Why belief is useful

If you think there's no way you could ever get behind the idea that there is more to the world around us than we can experience with our five senses (no matter how much we enhance them electronically or otherwise), let me reassure you that you don't have to. But it does make it more difficult:

There's a story of dubious origin that says that when the first European ships sailed into view on the American coast, the Native Americans weren't able to see them. The ships didn't figure in their previous experience, and so they weren't able to see them.

The story is probably a fabrication, but it points to a fact.

If you don't believe something is there, you can walk right past it and never see it.

Ever looked for something for ages and then realised that it was right there in front of you all the time?

Practise 6

Imagine a large corn field.

In the field are two people.

We'll call them Andrew and Beth.

Andrew and Beth have been told that somewhere in the field there's a £500 note.

They're both looking for it now, but Andrew doesn't believe the note's still there.

In fact, Andrew believes that it may never have even been there in the first place, and if it was, it was probably really a fiver, and the story just got exaggerated.

On the other hand, Beth has no doubt that the £500 note really is there, it just needs to be found, and so she's searching methodically and meticulously.

Who is most likely to give up searching first?

Who is most likely to mistake the note for a flower and walk right by it?

Who is most likely to enjoy the search and stick with it?

Who is most likely to walk away with the note?

Now let me re-iterate: it's perfectly possible to have a religious experience if you don't believe in religious experiences.

It's just bloody difficult.

What is belief?

A growing number of people use the word '*belief*' to talk about '***trusting blindly that an idea is correct without any proof***'.

I call that 'stupidity', not 'belief'.

The closest I've ever managed is '***accepting that something may well be so even though there is no proof***... but trusting blindly? That's insane!

Let me offer a different (though far from new) definition that the current militant atheist movement seems to have forgotten: my beliefs are the bits of information that work best when put to the test in the world.

I believe that when I flick the switch on the wall, the light will go on.

I have no way of proving it without actually doing it: the bulb may have blown or I might have forgotten to pay the electricity bill; but I believe that the light will go on because it's useful for me to.

I think that's a useful belief.

Imagine agonising every time you went to flick a switch just because the light *might* not turn on...

So this *belief* saves me time and worry.

So it's useful.

I act accordingly and confidently reach out for the switch when the room gets too dark. It normally works. Occasionally, very occasionally, I'm disappointed, and the bulb gets changed.

How do we form beliefs?

Let's take this example a little bit further.

I developed this belief about switches and lights by observing it work for other people as a small child.

I spent some time trying it out for myself, repeatedly, much to my parents' annoyance; and finally, seeing that it worked most of the time, I adopted the belief.

Another example is the belief that bus 27 will turn up at my bus stop at 7:24am to take me to work.

I have no proof that it will until it does actually arrive; (in fact my belief has been proven wrong enough times for me to consider purchasing a car!) but it's useful for me to believe that it will because that belief makes sure I'm usually out of the house on time to catch it.

I developed this belief because the time-table told me it was so; I turned up one morning to put the claim to the test, and it worked. Over and over again for over five years now with only a few unavoidable let-downs.

So I believe it.

It's a useful belief.

I also believe that a sentient thing (being? force?) surrounds and permeates me and all things and that we can interact with it if we want to.

I believe that when I share my thoughts, worries, regrets, plans and gratitude with it, my life is made considerably better in ways that some would call coincidental.

Every time.

I used to believe that coincidences were due to blind luck which made them happen rarely. My belief that a Divine force is at work makes them happen often.

So I find the latter belief more useful than the former.

All this is purely self-serving. No duty involved here, just decisions based on what makes my life better.

If a belief doesn't have a useful purpose, why fight for it?

Note I didn't mention anything about this sentient thing being omnipotent or eternal, just because some religious people say it is.

How could they know and why would I want find out? What difference would it make?

What purpose would it serve for me to hold that belief?

It would just put me at odds with people who believe something else.

If it has no further purpose, why keep it?

If there's no way of knowing and no real consequence one way or the other, what's wrong with plain old *I don't know*?

Just because one belief works doesn't mean its companions do.

To summarise:

We form our beliefs by:

1) **getting information about how something works,**
2) **trying it out**
3) **rejecting whatever doesn't work out**
4) **and keeping anything that does.**

But we have to be methodical. It's easy to let two beliefs slip in together just because one of them works:

For example, just because I believe that Charles Darwin's description of evolution through natural selection is a good, coherent explanation for the origin of species; it doesn't mean that I believe that it can explain the origin of life (which it doesn't claim to!).

Another example:

Praying to win the lottery doesn't work.

It doesn't mean there's no God, it just means that *praying to win the lottery doesn't work.*

Praying to understand stuff I didn't use to understand does work.

It doesn't mean there *is* a God, it just means that *praying for better understanding works.*

Now when I pray, if I believe that I'm talking to something that's actually hearing, I get positive results. Whereas if I believe that I'm speaking to the walls I don't get any results at all.

So I believe that I am speaking to a sentient mind, Because it works better.

Practise 7

Here's another task for you, (you'll need to grab that pen and paper again).

Think carefully about anything you think you know about 'God' or 'the Divine' or the spiritual realm or whatever you feel comfortable calling it.

Now assess whether it's a belief you have tested, bought into without proof, or simply rejected because you felt that you couldn't keep this one thing without also accepting a whole host of insane nonsense that went with it...

1) Write a list of everything you think people believe about God.
2) Next to each listing, write a T+ next to every belief that you've tried out and has come up with positive results and T- for anything you've tried out with no success.
3) Write a 'P!' next to everything that's possible but you haven't put it to the test yet or haven't observed whether the world-model that it implies works.
4) Write a 'U' next to everything that <u>would</u> be useful to your life if it turned out to work.

5) Write a 'W' next to any belief which would appear to be worthless at least at first glance, stuff that would make no difference to your life one way or another.
6) You can have more than one letter next to each belief.
7) Keep the list in a safe place for future reference.

Step 5

KEEP IT SECRET

One of the teachings that I was surprised to find in the New Testament goes like this (see if you can spot the bit that most Christians seem to have overlooked...):

"Be careful not to practice your righteousness in front of others to be seen by them. If you do, you will have no reward from your Father in heaven.

"So when you give to the needy, do not announce it with trumpets, as the hypocrites do in the synagogues and on the streets, to be honoured by others. Truly I tell you, they have received their reward in full. But when you give to the needy, do not let your left hand know what your right hand is doing, so that your giving may be in secret. Then your Father, who sees what is done in secret, will reward you.

(Now pay particular attention to this next bit...)

"And when you pray, do not be like the hypocrites, for they love to pray standing in

the synagogues and on the street corners to be seen by others. Truly I tell you, they have received their reward in full. But when you pray, go into your room, close the door and pray to your Father, who is unseen. Then your Father, who sees what is done in secret, will reward you. And when you pray, do not keep on babbling like pagans, for they think they will be heard because of their many words. Do not be like them, for your Father knows what you need before you ask him. [...]

(Amazing, right? I mean, isn't that precisely the opposite of what we associate most religions with? And he continues...)

"When you fast, do not look sombre as the hypocrites do, for they disfigure their faces to show others they are fasting. Truly I tell you, they have received their reward in full. But when you fast, put oil on your head and wash your face, so that it will not be obvious to others that you are fasting, but only to your Father, who is unseen; and your Father, who sees what is done in secret, will reward you."

Matthew 6:1-18 (NIV)

So, did you spot the bit that gets overlooked?

That's right... all of it! From beginning to end!

I can't tell you how surprised I was the first time I read this.

Actually, among all the teachings attributed to Jesus in the New Testament, I never found a single suggestion that organised religion was a good idea.

The opposite crops up pretty regularly though... there are plenty of recommendations not to trust what others say about God, but to nurture a direct relationship.

If we are all so unique, how can another's path be right for you?

Of course it's a good idea to have examples of how things have panned out for other people, but to mimic every aspect of someone else's divine encounter isn't the same as having a divine encounter yourself...

Lock the door

So it turns out that a church, mosque, synagogue, temple or gurdwara aren't the ideal place to have a divine experience.

The ideal place is wherever you can be *alone* with no risk of being interrupted or somebody walking in.

A place with a lock on the door, a place where you feel comfortable.

Prayer is as intimate as it gets.

Anyone watching means you'll be self-conscious.

Even someone close.

How can you let yourself go into the experience if you're worried about how mad you'd look to an onlooker?

Solitude.

It really is the only way.

If you can't have a little privacy in your own home, I find that a short walk somewhere out of the way usually does the trick.

It helps if there's a nice natural scenery to look at.

I don't know why, it just seems to work better.

Like in the woods or by the sea or on the downs.

Pray out loud, not in your head

One of the reasons why secrecy and solitude are recommended is because when you start out, praying out loud works better.

Sure, the Divine would 'hear' if you only thought your prayers in your head instead of pronouncing them, but I'm not recommending praying out loud for God's benefit. I'm recommending it for yours.

Speaking out loud helps us concentrate on what we're saying.

It's easier to hold a trail of thought, to follow it to its natural conclusion, sometimes words come out that we weren't expecting.

That's always interesting to notice.

Sometimes we hear our situation put into words and the solution suddenly becomes clear.

You're good enough to pray

OK, I hear you say, but now that it comes to it, I'm not sure I want to speak to God. I mean I've done so many bad things...

In Matthew 7:12-2, Jesus says:

"Do not judge, or you too will be judged. For in the same way you judge others, you will be judged, and with the measure you use, it will be measured to you."

God is only as judgemental as you are.

God is NOT as judgemental as your parents, friends, teachers, local policeman, or religious fanatic.

Practise 8

1) Over the next few days, catch yourself judging. Others, yourself, situations, ideas, anything.

2) Make a note of how often it happens.

3) Realise that it's not God who judges and condemns us, it's ourselves.

When is a good time for prayer?

Any time you feel you can pray is the right time.

Some people say that praying on the loo is disrespectful. Or that you shouldn't pray if you're in any way intoxicated...

If you feel uncomfortable praying at those times, then don't.

Just know that it's you judging yourself, not the Divine which is with you at all times, even when you're on the loo or intoxicated!

If you're comfortable with it, God's comfortable with it.

If you're not comfortable with it, God's seen worse.

What does 'perfect' mean?'

God is supposed to be 'perfect'.

'Perfect' in my world doesn't mean judgemental and attached to 1940's values.

It's amazing how society has trained us to believe that 'perfect' is this nerd with a slick side-parting and top grades who tells on the cool guys who were happily smoking grass in the bushes.

That's not perfect, that's some kid with no friends.

God isn't some kid with no friends.

God is perfect.

Perfect means you'd be happy to spend the rest of time with it.

So, once again, we're not talking about your parents' idea of perfect or your old teachers' ideas of perfect, we're talking about your own idea of perfect.

That's what you're talking to.

What to pray about?

Prayer is a conversation with the Universe of which you are a part. It knows you inside and out, so there are no taboos, no topics out of bounds.

So if deep down you're embarrassed about aspects of your life, bring it up. Say how you feel about it and let things start from there. You've got the door closed, right? So it's strictly confidential!

If there's stuff you do that you don't see the harm in and that actually makes lives more enjoyable, then why would God have a problem with that?

Thank God for it instead of worrying about what God might think about it... God's not your mum!

Practise 9

The time you've been waiting for has arrived:

1) Find a place where you're comfortable, alone and where it would be impossible or near impossible for you to be over-heard or interrupted. (Chose a time when it's also ok to turn off your mobile phone)

2) Consider that you're going to acknowledge the presence of something which has always been with you, but you have never experienced. Maybe prepare yourself and the place you're in accordingly (imagine the kind of thing you'd do if you were about to meet one of your parents for the first time ever – would a shower be in order? Light a candle? Make the place smell nice?)

3) Perform your favourite hypothalamus-inhibiting exercise from Step 3. Sing, chant, breath, whatever works. For at least 5 minutes.

4) Now get yourself comfortable.

5) In your own time, speak out. Anything that comes to your head is ok. If you're thinking it, say it out loud. Just speak your mind. No bargaining that 'if you give me a sign I'll believe in you' or anything like that, instead, just say whatever you actually want to say to God knowing that God is listening. If it's a rant about how hard it is to believe, then say it. Ask why it is so. If you want to apologise for something, do. If it's gratitude you want to express, express it.

And then keep going. Anything you want to say is ok. Contrary to what the religious type believe, God doesn't get offended. That wouldn't be perfect.

Just enjoy the chat. For as long as you want.

I'll let you get on with it now.

Enjoy.

WARNING

As a word of warning before you start the next step, may I strongly recommend that you complete the exercise in step 5 regularly over a sustained period of time (A week? A month or two?) before attempting this.

This step may just seem a little difficult otherwise.

Though of course you do what you feel is right... It really is just a recommendation.

See you then!

Step 6

SURRENDER

You're back?

I hope you're enjoying your new skill, you must be full of questions, but by now you're probably addressing them to the source rather than to some interpreter. Isn't that more satisfying?

Aren't the answers more useful?

And personal?

And relevant?

Good.

Now's the time for our next step.

'Surrender' is a more accurate word than 'Submission'

People of various traditions and faiths often use the word 'submission'.

I think the word 'submission' is the wrong word for what we're about to explore.

'Submission' is a master vs. slave word. It's something a serf does, something a Tyrant demands.

That's not what this step is about at all, and I think that people who use it are just repeating a mis-translation without having experienced what it's supposed to point to.

Let me try to give you an idea of what we are actually talking about here.

Picture yourself in the following scenario:

You're on a hiking holiday in the mountains. You set out early in the morning having packed your lunch and water flask. It's very early morning when you leave and the sky is cloudy and you can feel the cold wind on your face.

You make good headway in the morning, but by lunch time the weather turns really bad, first a drizzle, but soon it's sheets of rain that quickly turns to sleet in the cold.

You are drenched to the bone and frozen.

You turn to head home, but you don't recognise where you are on the map. You're out of food, your phone has run out of battery, you walk and walk till your muscles burn.

At last you find a familiar path and make your way home.

You open your front door, exhausted, drop your bag and change your clothes. After a good hearty dinner, you run yourself a hot bath.

Now, do you 'submit' to that bath?

No.

You surrender.

You let it take over.

You're quite happy to let it do the work for the while.

You don't begrudge it, you're actually very grateful.

Your muscles relax and it feels great.

That's the kind of surrender that I'm talking about here.

Not submission at all.

Surrendering to God is even more rewarding, only much, much less easy because you can see and feel your bath; God, as we have seen, is experienced with senses we usually forget about.

Remembering that we have more than five senses

As you have been experiencing over the past few weeks, we don't use our usual five external senses to experience the Divine. We don't see, hear, taste, smell or touch the Divine, and yet we sense the Divine's presence.

The trouble is, with a fully functioning hypothalamus, it's not easy to remember that there is more to reality beyond the fragment which we sense with our basic five.

There's this great Proverb that goes like this:

Trust in the LORD with all your heart
  and lean not on your own understanding;
in all your ways submit to him,
  and he will make your paths straight.

Proverbs (3:5-6)

If you can forgive the language for a while and just replace that 'LORD' with 'the Divine' or whatever other phrase you feel more comfortable with, and swap 'submit' for 'surrender', you have an excellent maxim by which to live for the next couple of weeks.

Try it out.

See if it works.

Let God take over.

See where it leads you.

It works

Here's a nice story that happened to me as a student a few weeks after that first encounter that you witnessed me having in the Introduction.

This one experience was the first of many of its kind, but I often refer to it because it was my first and it had huge implications for the rest of my life.

You'll remember that my campus happened to be located in the armpit of the world known to the locals as Clacton-on-sea. Let me tell you a bit more about this charming place. Clacton-on-sea was a tiny seaside resort whose inhabitants hated us students and usually let us know with the aid of knives and knuckledusters.

The two highlights of the town were:

1) The McDonald's in the town centre, and

2) the boy racers who would cruise round and round and round the McDonald's from dawn till dawn, tirelessly displaying their Fiestas and Escorts for our appreciation.

Needless to say that any opportunity I had to escape, I took.

So this one day, I realised that I had £30 left before hitting my overdraft limit.

And a week to go before my allowance got wired over from France where my parents lived.

So I did the only sensible thing: I decided to get a return ticket to London.

Obviously.

It wasn't *very* far, and by the time I'd paid for my student tickets, I had just a little under £20 left.

I had an amazing time: I went straight to Piccadilly Circus where I was hoping to buy cheap theatre tickets. (I didn't know about Leicester square, what can I say?)

The Criterion claimed to sell cheap tickets from 1pm, so to use the time, I went to the Trocadero.

At the time, it featured an IMAX cinema which was showing Fantasia 2000 (giving you an idea of when this happened, eh?) so a ticket to see that was £8, leaving me with just enough for a sandwich, before hitting the £10 I needed for the theatre ticket.

I was back at the Criterion by one, and the ticket I bought was for the Reduced Shakespeare Company, performing all of Shakespeare's works in an hour. Great! I thought. That means I'll definitely catch the last train home.

I then took off for the Tate galleryin Pimlico and gorged myself with free culture. The show time arrived, and I sat in the back row, all smug, only to realise that the one hour thing wasn't an hour at all! What with the interval, (of course), the messing around in between scenes and the encores, (the public wants their money's worth, don't they?) it was getting very close to my last train's departure time.

The curtain went down and I was out of my seat in a flash, rushing past the slow-moving crowds.

I ran out of the theatre and into the Underground train, checking my watch all the way to Liverpool Street, my heart sinking a little more with each second as this slug-tube crept forward.

I got to Liverpool Street station already knowing that I'd missed the train. The departures boards confirmed it.

There was one more direct train to Colchester (which is one of the stops on the way to Clacton-on sea).

Maybe I could catch up with the train I'd missed, and change at Colchester.

I took my seat and waited forever for the train to depart. The doors closed and the train finally started. On and on the journey went, every station seeming like an eternity. Would I catch up the Clacton train? I prayed. It calmed me. For the first time I asked God for something: I asked to catch the Clacton train up.

The train finally pulled into Colchester station. The controller's voice warned that this was the terminal and everybody should get off.

I didn't need telling. I could see the Clacton train on the next platform! The train slowed down for what seemed like an eternity.

We'd caught up the Clacton train! My prayer had come true!

But something was wrong.

My train finally came to a complete halt and I was pushed the 'open' button on the door repeatedly until it finally hissed open.

I leapt out and ran as hard as I could to the bridge, only to hear the Clacton train's doors bleep their shrill alarm and whoosh shut. I didn't stop running. I heard the unmistakable sigh of the wheels grinding to a start on the tracks.

I still ran.

Down the stairs, heart thumping.

I banged on the side of the moving train with my hand as it gathered speed and finally disappeared into the distance leaving nothing but silence, cold, and the awareness that I was stranded without a mobile phone, without a penny, without a map, without a clue where to go or what to do.

I felt exactly the way you can imagine.

It was past midnight. And it was freezing. I was wearing jeans and a fashionable shirt. No coat, not even a sweater.

The conductor came up to me: 'We're closing up now, please make your way to the exit.'

I told him I'd missed my train, and asked if I could please spend the night on one of their benches.

He looked a bit concerned: 'Sorry, son, not allowed to lock anyone in, you'll have to find somewhere else. I wish I could help.'

I nodded and made my way to the exit.

I remember coming out onto the deserted street and thinking: 'I'm going to have to walk to Clacton.' And then immediately realising I didn't even know which direction to turn to do that.

I prayed. I prayed for a sign. I would start walking in a random direction, and God would give me a sign of some sort.

Anything.

I set off on what promised to be a very long walk.

Within two minutes of walking, I came to a road sign. Clacton-on-sea, it said.

16 miles.

I took a deep breath and set off.

I soon came to a main road. It was mainly deserted now, but the odd car was still driving by.

Every time I heard one approaching I would put my thumb out and don my most charming smile, but no-one stopped. Not a great time of the day for hitch-hiking...

One o'clock came and went, two o'clock, I just kept on walking, telling myself that if I could just keep on walking, I might not feel the cold so much.

By now there were hardly any cars at all. I'd seen maybe three in the last hour. None of them had stopped. I'd been praying all the way. I didn't understand. Was it all nonsense after all?

Something a friend in halls had told me came back to me. It had seemed arrogant at the time, but at this point, I was desperate. I'd try anything.

My friend had said that when you pray, you should be very precise, very *specific* if you're asking for something.

I had nothing to lose.

I asked God for a nice warm, large car, with a leather interior (I thought I might as well, in for a penny in for a pound, as they say) to stop within five minutes. The driver would be a reassuring, kind middle aged male. And a smoker. This may seem strange to want to be in a car that stinks of cigarettes, but my dad back in France smoked in his car and I thought the smell would make me feel like home. I thought it might be comforting.

Oh, and it had to have a decent sound system too.

I didn't quite chuckle because it wasn't really chuckling circumstances, but I cheered up no end just thinking about it.

Two minutes…

Three minutes…

Four minutes….

Four and a half…

Was that…?

Yes, in the distance, headlights coming over the hill. I walked up to the edge of the road and put my thumb out. The car approached. I shielded my eyes a little from the headlights. The car got closer, and closer and… drove straight past me.

And slowed down! My heart was racing. A wave of joy came over me like nothing I'd ever felt before. I ran up towards the car that had now stopped altogether a little way off. I ran and ran and…

My heart stopped. There was something written on the side of the car. A phone number. It was a Taxi. I resumed my sprint shaking my head, gesturing negative swipes with my hands. But the car wasn't moving. I finally reached the driver's window which was being wound down.

'I'm sorry!' I panted. 'I hadn't realised you were a Taxi!'

'It's ok, said the driver, a man in his mid forties maybe. Where are you heading?'

'I've got no money,' I repeated. 'I'm really sorry. Like, really, really no money. Honestly, I'm really sorry I made you stop.'

But he insisted. 'Where are you going?'

'Clacton.'

'Well, I've finished my shift anyway,' he said, 'I'm just on my way home now to Clacton. Hop in. It's fine.' he said.

I sometimes wonder if he really had finished or if he just took pity of a student who was down on his luck. Not that it would make any difference to how kind it was of him to offer to take me home.

I did hop in. Into his leather interior Mercedes. He had the radio playing softly. He drove off, but as he did so he checked me in the rear view mirror and asked politely if I would mind very much if he lit a cigarette, because it had been a long day.

I smiled and said that would be fine.

As we reached my halls of residence, the first hints of light were brightening the sky. I thanked the driver very profusely and asked him if he had a business card I could take to send him some money when my allowance came through. He just shook his head and told me that next time I saw a charity box for children, I should put a couple of quid in.

So I do. Every time I see one.

Practise 10

(Don't do this until you've established at least a semblance of a relationship with the Divine as described in Step 5, and have done so for some time.)

1) Pay attention over the next two weeks, and try to spot times when the Universe seems to be conspiring against you.

2) When such a time arises, notice your emotions. Anger is the most natural way to feel at these times.

3) To experience this very odd occurrence, just catch yourself feeling this anger and instead, pray.

4) Now relax and trust that the situation you're in is somehow to your benefit. If you feel like apologising for having lost your temper, do so in silent (whispered) prayer.

5) Now wait calmly and watch in amazement as that benefit is revealed.

It's usually spectacular. You're in for a surprise, so enjoy.

Do this as often as you can.

Not only when you're upset.

Find opportunities to let God take over, opportunities to allow God to do a better job than you or any human could do...

Don't forget to combine this with all of the preceding exercises. If you're finding it difficult to trust, to believe, do some breathing exercises to knock out that hypothalamus at least a bit... find something to be grateful for.

Use your new skills.

All of them.

They complement each other.

As they say in the teaching trade, 'Use it or lose it'.

The rest is up to you.

STEP 7

TAKING IT FURTHER

If you've been doing all the exercises, you should have a number of bits of paper lying about with various lists and thoughts jotted down on them.

Take them out now and see if any of it needs to be revised.

It's important to acknowledge that our understanding of how the Divine operates is never complete. You can't be filled if you already feel full enough, remember?

These lists you are holding will need constant revision. Some of it you will drop, some you will add to. Some you will have a complete change of mind about.

Regardless, the quest to fully understanding life is a fascinating one and one that can never be completely achieved.

Which is what I think makes it interesting.

Now that I interact with God, what's my religion?

It's a question I am often asked given my line of work, and one that I hate answering:

After all, did Noah have a religion?

Did Abraham?

No.

Yet according to the scriptures of three major world religions, they found 'favour in God's eyes'.

I hate labels.

The minute you announce that you're Christian or Muslim or Buddhist, or Jewish, people assume that you agree with everything that uses the same label. And they also assume that you must surely reject anything that comes under a *different* label.

Like this poor woman my sister was telling me about that she met at church who was sure homeopathy was from the devil. Though I'm sure she'd have lapped it up if it had been re-branded 'Christian medicine'.

It's just nonsense, isn't it? Labels, clubs...

I say if it works, use it, regardless of the label.

No, what if someone's not taking that as an answer? What if they're really pestering me because something without a label freaks them out?

I usually tell them I'm *Perennialist*.

This is a great answer because it usually ends the conversation right there: if they don't know what it means (and they never do), I tell them to look it up. End of story. Want to talk about the hypothalamus instead?

I like the idea of Perennialism because it keeps all doors open. You see, I've given you more than I usually give most people... look it up!

Why I stay away from set, organised forms of religion

Here are two quotations I'd like to share with you.

The first is from a 13th century mystic known for is his deeply insightful understanding of God.

This is one of the things he had to say on the matter:

> *'He who seeks God under settled form lays hold of the form, while missing the God concealed in it'*

Meister Eckhart

I'll just share this little passage from Matthew chapter 23 with you that you might like.

In this passage, Jesus is talking about the people officially responsible for helping other people experience God. Our modern-day cardinals, bishops and priests if you will.

Let's see what Jesus thought of them then and see if you think anything has changed since.

> *"Everything they do is done for men to see: They make their phylacteries wide and the tassels on their garments long; they love the place of honor at banquets and the most important seats in the synagogues; they love to be greeted in the marketplaces and to have men call them 'Rabbi.'*
>
> *"But you are not to be called 'Rabbi,' for you have only one Master and you are all brothers. And do not call anyone on earth 'father,' for you have one Father, and he is in heaven. Nor are you to be called 'teacher,' for you have one Teacher, the Christ. The*

greatest among you will be your servant. For whoever exalts himself will be humbled, and whoever humbles himself will be exalted.

'Woe to you, teachers of the law and Pharisees, you hypocrites! You shut the kingdom of heaven in men's faces. You yourselves do not enter, nor will you let those enter who are trying to.

Matthew 23

I think the same.

The common link

You remember the method we decided on for forming beliefs? You gather information, you try it out and if it works, you keep it until it's replaced by a better belief that works more often?

Well, the most useful way that I have found for gathering good quality information about God has been through reading scriptures and comparing them to each other to find the common links.

I use authorised texts and unauthorised texts too as the unauthorised ones have usually been rejected for political reasons and often hold much meatier material.

If they're available, why not use them?

Authorised scriptures are obvious: the Bible, the Qur'an, the Baghavad Gita, the Tao Te Ching, the Bodhicaryavatara and the Guru Grant Sahib are all worth a look.

If you're stuck for a place to start looking for unauthorised scriptures, you could use a popular search engine to look up the Nag Hammadi Library, it's a good starting point.

Once I've read the scripture, I compare it with what another scriptures say, always remembering that this is stuff that *people* have written about their own spiritual experiences, not God's 'actual words' as some people might claim.

Then I pick out the common points.

If there is disagreement, I think of ways in which the paradox can be reconciled, keeping in mind the political and power-hungry nature of humans.

If I can't make my mind up, I pray for guidance or I abandon both possibilities as unimportant details.

Anything else?

Yes! Plenty! But I promised to keep things basic and so this is as far as I take you in this book.

Just in case you want more, I'll leave you with a useful bibliography of books that use a similarly sensible approach to spirituality.

If you're looking for further weirdness, the books on the next page will completely mess with your world!

How far you want to take the experience is up to you.

BIBLIOGRAPHY

Author	Title(s)
Richard Rohr	- <u>Everything Belongs</u> - <u>Things Hidden</u>: *Scripture as Spirituality*
Aldous Huxley	- <u>The Doors of Perception</u> - <u>Heaven and Hell</u> - <u>The Perennial Philosophy</u>

Rupert Sheldrake	- <u>The Sense Of Being Stared At</u>:
	   and other aspects of the extended mind
	
	- <u>A New Science of Life</u>:
	   the hypothesis of Formative Causation

Seyyed Hossein Nasr	- <u>The Garden of Truth</u>: *the vision and promise of Sufism*
Jeremy Narby	- <u>The Cosmic Serpent</u>:

DNA and the origins of knowledge

Philip K Dick — Valis (novel)

Paramahansa Yogananda
- God Talks with Arjuna: *The Baghavad Gita*
- The Second Coming of Christ: *the resurrection of the Christ within you*

Robert Anton Wilson
- Prometheus Rising
- Quantum Psychology

Rick Strassmann
- DMT – The Spirit Molecule: *a doctor's revolutionary research into the biology of near-death and mystical experiences*

Huston Smith — Forgotten Truth

Rob Bell — Love Wins

Greg Egan — Quarantine (novel)

Dion Fortune — The Mystical Qabalah

Tau Malachi - <u>Living Gnosis:</u>
 A Practical guide to Gnostic Christianity